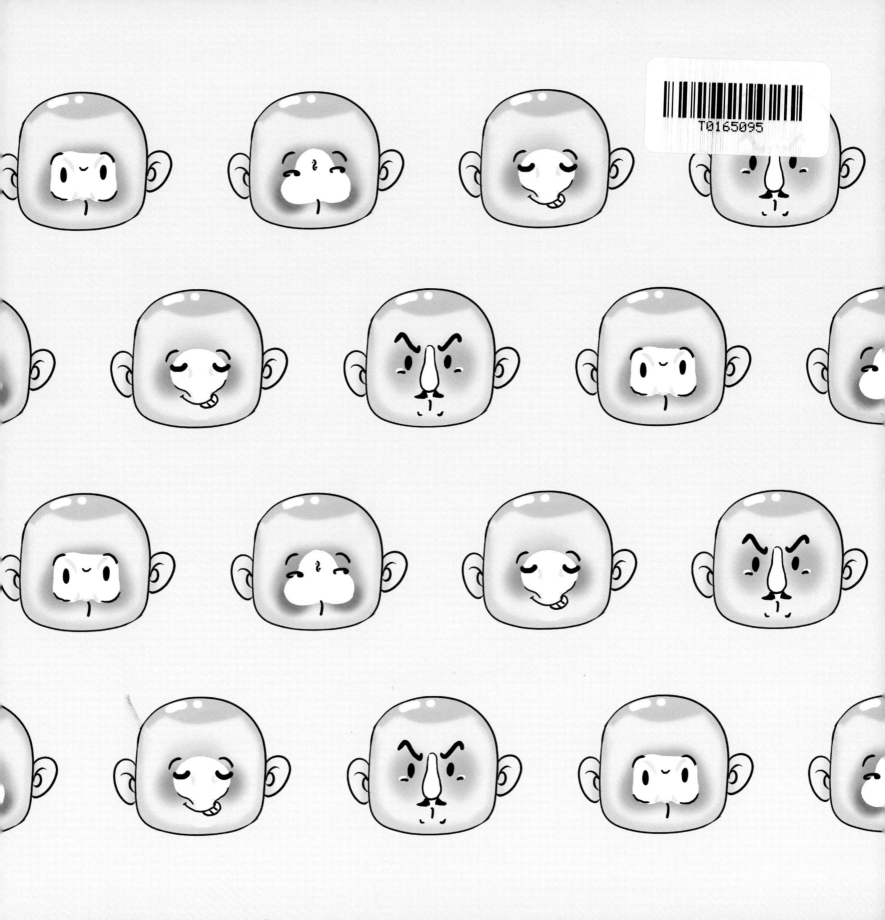

Introduction To Peking Opera

CHOU

By Zhou Chuanjia

Illustrated by Pangbudun'er

RC

Books Beyond Boundaries

ROYAL COLLINS

What is a *Chou*?

A *Chou* is a type of character in Peking Opera. Another name, roughly expressed in English, is "small painted face." These characters are usually humorous, funny, and bring people laughter.

Bar Tender

Yang Xiangwu

Shi Qian

Chong Gongdao

Vendor

Tang Qin

Qiu Xiaoyi

The county magistrate

Hu Jin

Woodcutter

Boatman

Secretary Wang

Jiang Gan

Innkeeper

Jiang Ping

Jin Xiangrui

Civil Chou

Civil *Chou* characters can be funny scholars or regular people.

Their faces can be like this:

Or this:

Or this:

Chou's beard in three locks

They have many different types of beard too.

Chou's mustache

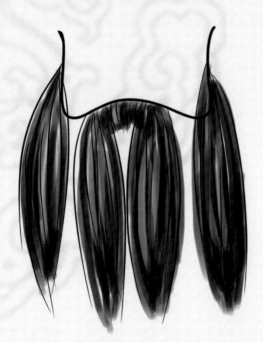

Chou's beard in four locks

Chou's beard in five locks

Lotus Leaf Headscarf

Floral *Xuezi* Robe for Civil *Chou*

Jiang Gan in *Talents' Gathering*

Feather Fan

When a resourceful figure carries a feather fan, he'll look handsome and confident. But someone like Secretary Wang looks funny and ridiculous with it.

High Square Headscarf

"Gilded Robe"

This robe is full of stiches and patches. You can tell that whoever wears it does not have much money.

Secretary Wang in *Comedy in the Bridal Chamber*

9

Jin Xiangrui in *The Precious Rouge Gown*

Tang Qin in *Martyr and Revenge*

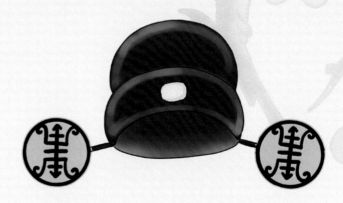

Gauze Cap

The wings on the gauze cap for *Chou* characters have two circular decorations at each end.

Official Robe

Hu Jin in *Cunning Maid*

The county magistrate in
Five Mischievous Goblins

Square Official Boots

11

Martyr and Revenge

The *Martyr and Revenge* is one act from the play *Jade Cup*.

During Emperor Jiajing's reign (1522-1566). Mo Huaigu, a court minister, helped and supported a poor student called Tang Qin. But Tang Qin was an ungrateful man; he knew Mo Huaigu had a precious jade cup that his family had owned for generations and wanted to butter up a higher-ranked official by giving this cup to him. Mo Huaigu, of course, didn't agree to this. Tang Qin was angry and said some bad things about him in front of the higher-ranked official. The official believed him and decided to kill Huaigu.

Huaigu had a loyal servant called Cheng who looked exactly like him. Knowing his master was in danger, Cheng committed suicide and made everyone think it was Huaigu who died. But the devious Tang Qin was not so easily fooled. The judge Lu Bing discovered what Tang Qin really wanted was to marry Huaigu's concubine Xueyan. Therefore, he pretended to grant Tang's wish but simultaneously secretly told Xueqin to kill this evil man. On their wedding day, Tang Qin was very excited and drank a lot of wine. As soon as he fell asleep, Xueqin stabbed him with a sword and killed him. After this, she killed herself too to show her love and faith for Huaigu.

There are two main themes in this act: the first is "identifying the martyr," which shows Tang Qin and Lu Bing working out whether the murdered man is Huaigu or not. The second is "taking revenge," which shows Xueyan killing Tang Qin for the death of Cheng.

13

Chou Characters in Short Jackets

These are the most commonly seen *Chou* characters. They wear a short blue jacket called a *chayi*. They are usually common people of the lower class.

Short Jacket

Felt Hat

Bar Tender

Vendor

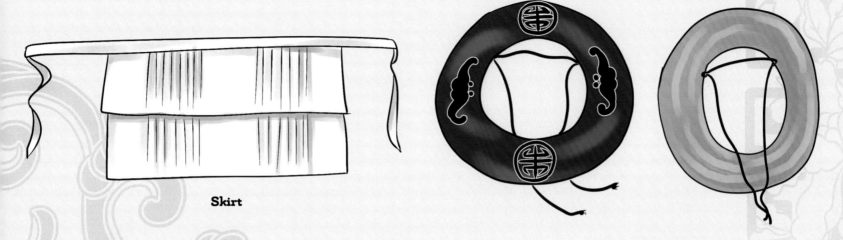

Skirt

Visor of Straw Hats

Woodcutter

Boatman

15

The *Chou* characters have a special fun performance called the "short act." The actors need to remain squatting while they perform in order to show the characters they're playing are very short. The typical character played in this way is Wu Dalang the bun seller.

The actor's regular height.

The actor's height when doing the "short act."

"Fresh buns!"

Chou Characters in Headdress

This is another type of *Chou* character aside from the "square headscarf" and the "short jacket." The acting of these *Chou* characters is more serious than that of short-jacket *Chou*s.

Small Nomad's Hat

Blue Archery Cloak

Chong Gongdao in *Su San Under Escort*

Flats

Zhezi Robe

Duck-Tail Headdress

Innkeeper at the _Lucky Inn_

19

Story of the Black Pot

In the Song dynasty (10th–13th century), there was a rich businessman named Liu Shichang. One day, he went on a business trip. On his way back, it started to rain so he sought shelter in Zhao Da's home. Da was greedy and he wanted Shichang's money. At night, when Shichang was asleep, Da killed him and burned his body into ashes. Then he mixed the ashes with mud and buried it in a small black pot. Later, a poor old man Zhang Huaigu, who once lent some money to Da, came. Da didn't want to pay his debt so he gave the black pot to Huaigu instead.

After the old man left Da's home, the spirit of Shichang appeared from the pot and told his tragic story. He then begged Huaigu to take him to Lord Bao and take revenge for his death. So, Huaigu brought the pot to Lord Bao's court, and the honest and virtuous judge arrested Da and sentenced him to death.

Colorful *Dans*

These characters are also called "ugly wenches." They are female characters who might not be especially good looking but who are definitely humorous and hilarious. Usually, these roles are played by male actors.

"The Colorful *Dan* characters always amuse the audience and lighten up the play's atmosphere."

Cheng Xueyan in *The Perfect Match*

Matchmaker Liu in *Picking up the Jade Bracelet*

Maid Biyu in *Qilin Purse*

22

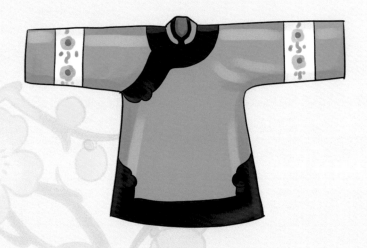

Colorful _Dan_'s Top

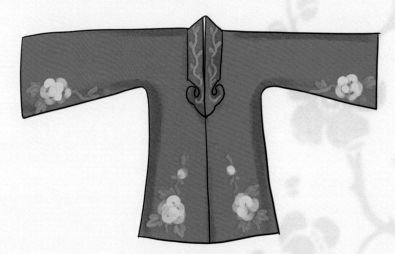

Dress for Women

Silk Flowers

Embroidered Shoes

Long Waistcoat

Short Waistcoat

The Perfect Match

Minister Cheng Pu had two daughters, Xueyan and Xue'e. The younger daughter was very beautiful, but her older sister was not so fortunate.

Once, on their father's birthday, the son of a family friend called Mu Juyi came to celebrate with them. Juyi was very handsome and Mr. Cheng wanted to marry his second daughter to him. But the older girl went secretly to Juyi's room at night. Thinking she was Xue'e, Juyi was shocked by her look and indecency to meet with men at night. So, he decided not to pull out of this marriage and left the house.

There was an ugly man called Zhu Qiansui who had always wanted to marry the beautiful Xue'e. Now that Juyi was gone, he thought to himself: "Wonderful! I will pretend to be Juyi and marry the beauty. No one will know." However, the girls' mother wanted her eldest daughter to marry Juyi, so she asked Xueyan instead of Xue'e to get into the wedding sedan chair. The fake groom and the fake bride were both astonished to see each other. They couldn't understand what was going on. Qiansui said: "The Ms. Cheng I want is a beautiful little maiden, who is this ugly old wench?" While Xueyan said, "The Mr. Mu I want is a handsome young fellow, who is this weird old clown?" But they were already married to each other and they couldn't do anything about it anymore.

Later, old Mr. Cheng met Juyi again during a fight against some bandits. Xue'e also came to the frontier to visit her father. Mr. Cheng was very happy and decided to marry her to Juyi. But Juyi thought it was the vulgar girl again, so he kept saying no. But Mr. Cheng persuaded him and brought him to the wedding chamber. Sitting there, was the fine and decent Xue'e. Juyi was of course very happy to see her, and they married immediately in the camp.

Martial Chou

These characters are also called "speakers and jumpers." The actors are very good at jumping and they perform a lot of martial arts on stage.

This is what facial makeup for Martial *Chou* characters looks like:

Mustache for Martial *Chou:*

Mustache in one lock

Mustache in two locks

Mane Hat

Top Headdress

Fish Scale Shoes

They often wear hats of these styles:

Tight Shirt and Tight Pants

***Xuezi* Robe for Martial *Chou* Characters**

There are many heroic outlaw figures who are Martial *Chou* characters. They are very skillful fighters, and they rob the rich and use the money to help the poor.

Yang Xiangwu in *Stealing the Nine-Dragon Cup*

Qiu Xiaoyi in *Stealing the Silver Flagon*

Jiang Ping in *Shattering the Copper Net Array*

Shi Qian in *Stealing the Chain Mail*

29

Stealing the Chain Mail

This is a story from *Water Margin*.

The great general Huyan Zhuo fought against the outlaws at Liangshan Marsh with his chain-linked armored cavalry formation. At this critical moment, one of the hero bandits called Tang Long "The Leopard" suggested seeking help from Xu Ning – the only person who could shatter the cavalry formation. But it was impossible. Xu Ning was an imperial military commander. How could he ever agree to help the outlaws fight against the court? Finally, the strategist Wu Yong came up with an idea. He sent Shi Qian, a very skilled thief, to steal the precious chain mail from Xu Ning's house.

Shi Qian crept into Xu's house at night and took away the chain mail hanging on the roof with extraordinary stealth. When Xu found out that the chain was missing, he followed Shi Qian all the way to Liangshan Marsh, where the hero bandits persuaded him to help them. In the end, Xu shattered the cavalry formation and defused the crisis for the warriors in the Marsh.

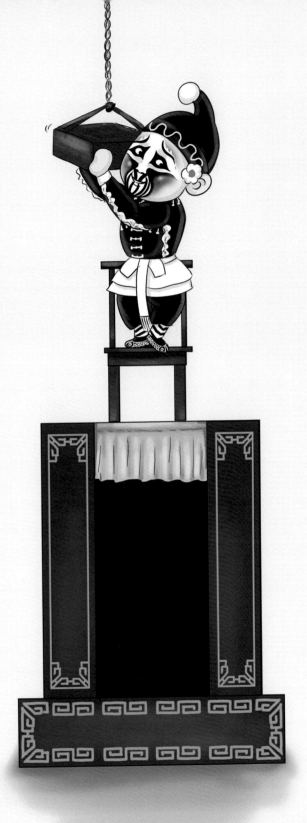

Stealing the Silver Flagon

Zhang Ding lost an important silver flagon owned by the military commander-in-chief. The commander believed he must have stolen it and forced him to pay for the loss. Ding had no money and did not know what to do; in the end, he had no choice but to sell his daughter to a businessman, who was actually a foreign spy in disguise.

The silver flagon was indeed stolen by someone. His name was Qiu Xiaoyi and he was a highly skilled thief known by his nickname, "snitch." When he heard the Zhang family was in distress, he drove away the fake businessman and brought Zhang's daughter back. Then, he went with Zhang to return the flagon to the commander-in-chief. The commander was very impressed by Qiu's capability and righteous character, so he decided to give him another chance. He asked Qiu to steal the flagon from the mansion again and Qiu accomplished this task as successfully as he did the first time. The commander was delighted and forgave him for stealing. Qiu was allowed to open an inn outside the military camp and he worked as an innkeeper ever since.

Protecting the Protected

The great general Jiao Zan killed an evil but powerful figure by accident so the emperor banished him to a faraway land. His commander-in-chief Yang Yanzhao was afraid that he would run into trouble on his way. Yang thus sent another officer called Ren Tanghui to secretly go with Jiao and protect him if needed. When Jiao was escorted to an inn at Sanchakou, the innkeeper Liu Lihua wanted to rescue Jiao from his banishment. But when he was about to enter Jiao's room at night, Ren thought he was going to kill him, so he broke in and started fighting Liu in the dark. Finally, Jiao entered and stopped the fight. The misunderstanding was cleared and the three became good friends.

Let's learn more about Peking Opera (4)

Zhou Chuanjia – professor at Beijing Union University and researcher at the Central Research Institute of Culture and History.

The *Chou* category

The facial makeup for *Chou* characters features a square piece of white paint on and around the nose. We also refer to these characters as "small painted face" or "third-class painted face." The *Chou* characters are mostly humorous, clownish, vulgar, or dishonorable with their conduct. There are no fixed roles in this category. A *Chou* can be either a man or a woman from all walks of life – from emperors and military commanders to regular people doing various jobs. They can be good or evil, smart or foolish, loyal or ungrateful. All these characters are different.

The performance of civil *Chou* characters is fun and the actors tell a lot of jokes to lighten the play's atmosphere. Different characters will wear distinctive costumes based on the status of the roles. We can divide them into several sub-categories by their outfit and other personal features. There is "the square headscarf," "the cap and belt," "the *xuezi* robe," "the short jacket," "the old," "the archery cloak," "the commoner," and "the female."

Chou characters in the square headscarf wear a square headscarf as well as *xuezi* robe and silk belt. These are usually students, scholars, or strategists, like Jiang Gan in *The Talents' Gathering*, Tang Qin in *The Jade Cup*, Zhang Wenyuan in *Tragedy in the Chamber Upstairs* and Li Gu in *Liangshan Bandits Rescue Their Friend*.

Chou characters in cap and belt are also called official *Chous*. They wear helmet headdresses, dragon robes, or other official robes. The roles they depict are usually emperors, kings, generals, high ministers, and magistrates. For example, King Min of Qi in *Fugitive Prince*, Duke Jing of Qi in *Murder at the Xiangjiang Feast*, Duke Ling of Jin in *The Orphan of Zhao*, Bo Pi in *Bewitching Beauty*, Gao Lishi in *The Drunken Beauty*, Cheng Yaojin in *General Selected by All*, Jin Xiangrui in *The Scheme for Finding the Lost Seal*, Huang Wenbing in *The Crisis at the Xunyang Hotel*, and Wu Dapao in *The Five Mischievous Goblins*.

Chou characters in *xuezi* robes wear a winged headscarf and an embroidered robe. These are usually rich and frivolous playboys, like Gao Shide in *Yezhu Forest*, young Master Yang in *Stealing the Royal Token*, and Shi Wen in *Teahouse Romance*.

Chou characters in short jackets, as indicated by the name, wear short tops and a waist bag. They are common people of the lower class, like Zhang Gudong in *The Idler Miscalculates*, Zhang Yi in *the Golden Turtle Took the Bait*, Wu Yanneng in *Biting the Hand that Feeds*, and the tub fixer in *Fixing the Evil Container for the Drought Demon*.

Old *Chous*, of course, are the elders in a play. They have special makeup and wear white beards to show their age. Characters in the Old *Chou* sub-category include Zhang Biegu in *Story of the Black Pot*, Wang Laohao in *The Deprived General Sells His Horse*, Chong Gongdao in *Su San Under Escort*, and the woodcutter in *The Woodcutter Guide*.

The identities of *Chou* characters in archery cloaks are more varied. They can be dukes and military officers, but they can be soldiers and servants too. Eunuchs, captains, directors, retainers, policemen, police officers, escort guards, and pages can also wear this outfit. The archery cloak has different styles, such as dragon, silk, and linen cloaks. Actors can wear a waistcoat or a soldier's jacket over the cloak depending on their roles. Characters include Jia Gui in *Fu Peng's Trial*, Mu Gua in *The Goddess of War*, Luan Bu in *Palace Coup for Throne*, Xia Houen in *Changban Hills*, the policemen in *Fugitive Prince*, and Hua An in *Battle of Taiping*.

The common *Chous* are regular people but with a more specific occupation, like innkeepers, doctors, Buddhist monks, and Daoist priests. Instead of short jackets, they usually wear long robes. Examples are the innkeeper in *Lucky Inn*, Dr. Liu in *Quack Doctor*, Zhang Nianyou and Duan Yiren in *Two Fake Monks*.

The female *Chou*, or colorful *Dan*, usually represents old female characters in a play. There is: matchmaker Liu in *Picking up the Jade Bracelet*, the sorceress in *Summer Snow*, nanny Jia in *The Henpecked Husband Turns into Sheep*, granny Chen in *Qilin Purse*, Mrs. Chen in *Teahouse Romance*, Mrs. Dou in *Gold Token*, and village woman Mrs. Hu in *In-laws' Fight*.

These characters have little makeup, but the colorful *Dan* characters are different. They represent much younger figures and usually put on very heavy makeup, like Sai Xishi in *Ms Rescuer*, Cheng Xueyan in *The Perfect Match*, and Mrs. Yu in *Bewitching Beauty*.

As for Martial *Chous*, these actors not only have to perform martial arts but also need to be articulate when delivering dialogues. We call them "speak and jump" because these are the two skills required. The characters in this sub-category are often heroic outlaws and skilled fighters who are quick-witted, fluent in speech, good at fighting, and humorous. For example, there is Liu Lihua in *Protecting the Protected*, Hu Li in *Enemy Becomes Family*, Jia Liang in *Rescue the Captive Minister*, and some famous thieves and bandits. They are Yang Xiangwu in *Stealing the Nine-Dragon Cup*, Zhu Guangzu in *Stealing the Double Hooks*, Qiu Xiaoyi in *Stealing the Silver Flagon*, Hu Che'er in *Stealing the Double Spears*, Shi Qian in *Stealing the Chain Mail*, *Robbing the Royal Tomb*, and *Stealing the Chicken*. Some people say that "speak and jump" chous actually belong to a different sub-category from the Martial *Chou*. While "speak and jump" emphasizes both martial performances and dialogues, Martial *Chou* characters focus only on the performances. For example, Qin Ren in *Damsel in Distress*, Feng Hong in *Yu Qian Saves His Master*, the "Strong-Leg Tiger" in *White Water Beach*. Also, the Martial *Chou* characters are trained for the Monkey King's performances. In comparison to other roles in Peking Opera, dialogues are exceptionally important to the *Chou* characters. Aside from doing the *Jing* dialogue, *Yun* dialogue, and *Jing-Yun* dialogue, they also need to learn dialects from Suzhou, Yangzhou, Shanxi, Shandong, Hejian, Henan, Huizhou, Shaoxing, etc.

Each of the four Peking Opera roles – *Sheng*, *Dan*, *Jing*, and *Chou* – has a group of characters tailored for it and can only be played by actors and actresses trained for this role. The division is clearly defined. Generally, we call actors playing the characters tailored for their own roles "original adepts." Every role has its original adept plays. But sometimes, actors and actresses in one role will play the characters of another role. For example, a *Sheng* actor may play a character in the *Dan*, Martial *Jing*, or *Chou* categories. These cases are called "playing a breeches role." Because the obligations of actors and actresses vary, in some plays it is a tradition for one actor to play two different characters. We call them "one in two," "one in three," or "one horse for two generals," "one horse for three generals."

About the Author:

Zhou Chuanjia was born in 1944. He studied at Peking University and Chinese National Academy of Arts, where he received his doctorate in literature. Zhou is a professor at Beijing Union University, a researcher at the Central Research Institute of Culture and History, and an expert who enjoys the special allowance of the State Council. Zhou has been teaching and researching Chinese literature, opera history, and opera critique for a long time. His major publications include *Introduction to Opera Script Writing*, *Performance of Famous Dan Actors*, and *Opera: Chinese Cultural Elements*.

About the Illustrator:

Pangbudun'er is an independent writer and painter of the post-80s generation. His work is engaging with its own unique style. He painted illustrations for *Fun Talks on the Three Kingdoms* by Cai Kangyong and Hou Wenyong; his other publications include *Raising the Curtains: Will you Hear Some Peking Opera?* and several Peking Opera picture books such as *Protecting the Protected* and *Empty Fort Strategy*.

Introduction To Peking Opera:
Chou

By Zhou Chuanjia
Illustrated by Pangbudun'er

First published in 2022 by Royal Collins Publishing Group Inc.
Groupe Publication Royal Collins Inc.
BKM Royalcollins Publishers Private Limited

Headquarters: 550-555 boul. René-Lévesque O Montréal (Québec) H2Z1B1 Canada
India office: 805 Hemkunt House, 8th Floor, Rajendra Place, New Delhi 110 008

Original Edition © Changchun Publishing House Co., Ltd.

ISBN: 978-1-4878-0914-0

To find out more about our publications, please visit www.royalcollins.com.